CW01024471

BRANCH LINE TO MORETONHAMPSTEAD

Vic Mitchell and Keith Smith

MP Middleton Press

First Published 1998
First reprint March 2006

ISBN 1 901706 27 3

© Middleton Press, 1998

Design   Deborah Esher
Typesetting   Barbara Mitchell

Published by
*   Middleton Press*
*   Easebourne Lane*
*   Midhurst, West Sussex*
*   GU29 9AZ*
Tel: 01730 813169
Fax: 01730 812601
Email: info@middletonpress.co.uk
www.middletonpress.co.uk

Printed & bound by Biddles Ltd, Kings Lynn

CONTENTS

INDEX

ACKNOWLEDGEMENTS

We are very grateful for the assistance received from so many of the photographers mentioned in the credits. We would also like to express our appreciation of the help given by P.G.Barnes, D.Clayton, G.Croughton, T.Heavyside, N.Langridge, Mr D. & Dr. S. Salter, N.Sprinks, G.T.V.Stacey, E.Youldon and our always helpful wives.

(Railway Clearing House 1917)

GEOGRAPHICAL SETTING

The Moretonhampstead branch followed the broad valley of the River Teign inland from its tidal limit at Newton Abbot for about three miles, towards Heathfield. It then ran along the narrowing valley of the River Bovey for about five miles and accompanied one of its tributaries for the final steep climb to the terminus, which was situated on the eastern flank of Dartmoor. There was a height gain of about 530ft.

The Teign Valley line ran north from Heathfield to Christow in that narrow and picturesque feature of the Devon landscape. North of the latter station, the line climbed out

of the valley and reached its summit between the two tunnels at Longdown before making a rapid descent into the Exe Valley, south of Exeter.

The geology of much of the area was of economic importance. Tin ores had been one of the reasons for proposing the line to Moretonhampstead but they ceased to be worked just before the route was opened. Barytes was mined and Granite and Basalt were quarried in the upper part of the Teign Valley. Ball Clay (a product of the decomposition of the former) has been won in large quantities in the district, it being loaded in the Heathfield area.

HISTORICAL BACKGROUND

The broad gauge Bristol & Exeter Railway reached the latter city on 1st May 1844. The route was extended by the South Devon Railway to Newton Abbot on 30th December 1846 and to Totnes on 20th July 1847. The route chosen was down the Exe Valley and along the coast. These companies bcame part of the Great Western Railway in 1876-78.

The Moretonhampstead & South Devon Railway was incorporated in 1862 and a service of broad gauge trains began running from Newton Abbot on 4th July 1866. They were operated by the SDR, which absorbed the line in 1872.

The Teign Valley Railway was the subject of no less than nine Acts between 1863 and its opening between Heathfield and Ashton on 9th October 1882. There was a mineral extension to Teignhouse near Christow. Being of standard gauge the line was isolated from the national system until May 1892, when the Moretonhampstead branch was converted from broad gauge.

The Exeter, Teign Valley & Chagford Railway received its Act in 1883, but the Chagford proposal was dropped in 1898 and the name was changed to the Exeter Railway. The line was opened on 1st July 1903, the GWR operating a train service between Heathfield and Exeter for the two companies. They became part of the GWR in 1923, which in turn became the Western Region of British Railways upon nationalisation in 1948.

Passenger service withdrawals were as follows: Heathfield to Exeter on 9th June 1958 and Newton Abbot to Moretonhampstead on 2nd March 1959. The route east of Christow was not used at all after closure to passengers. Freight facilities were withdrawn in stages, which are detailed in the captions.

PASSENGER SERVICES

In this table we refer to down trains that ran at least five days a week over the full length of the route. Some short workings are mentioned in the captions.

Most trains from Exeter terminated at Heathfield, but in the 1950s there was some through working to Newton Abbot. In the other direction, a few trains continued (unannounced) to Dulverton in that period. Similarly, some Moretonhampstead services originated at Paignton.

	Moretonhampstead branch		Teign Valley
	Weekdays	Sundays	Weekdays only
1869	4	2	-
1883	4	2	4
1904	6	2	5
1914	8	3	5
1924	10	2	6
1934	10	5	8
1944	6	-	5
1958	8	-	5

July 1914

1. Moretonhampstead branch

NEWTON ABBOT

1.   The first station was demolished in 1861 without photographic record. The east end of its successor is illustrated here, along with its gloomy footbridge under the roof. There were three through platforms but no bays. (Lens of Sutton)

The 1905 map has the London-Plymouth route from lower right to the left. Above it on the right is the Moretonhampstead branch; the single line passes over Whitelake Bridge just beyond the edge of the page.

2.   The west end of the second station is seen shortly before it was rebuilt in 1925-27. The map confirms that the two through lines on the right passed under a roof devoid of platforms. (Lens of Sutton)

3. The new station was officially opened on 11th April 1927, planning work having started in 1908. There were spacious facilities for passengers, four through platforms and one bay. The station had been simply "Newton" until 1877. (Lens of Sutton)

4. At about 6.45pm on 20th August 1940, German bombers reigned terror on unsuspecting civilians, killing 14, seriously injuring 29 and extensively damaging rolling stock. Some rails were tossed in the air and landed vertically through wagon floors. (British Rail)

Gt. Western Ry.   Gt. Western Ry.
MORETON   MORETON
HAMPSTEAD   HAMPSTEAD
            TO
NEWTON ABBOT
1/0½ PARLY.(3rd.Cls) 1/0½
Issued subject to the conditions & regu
lations set out in the Company's Time
Tables Books and Bills.   F.N)
Newton Abbot   Newton Abbot
7689

5. This and the following five pictures show trains at platform 9, the almost exclusive departure point for Moretonhampstead services. No. 1439 was recorded on 18th August 1953; about 70 locomotives were allocated to Newton Abbot at that time. (J.W.T.House/C.L.Caddy)

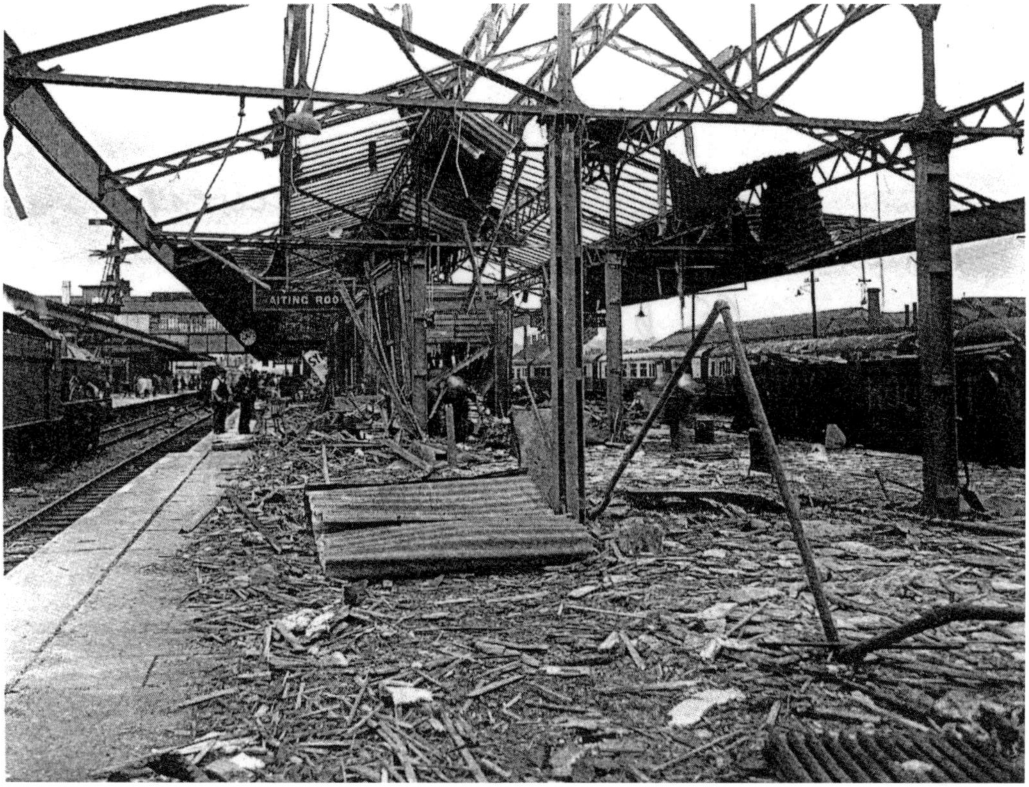
AITING ROO

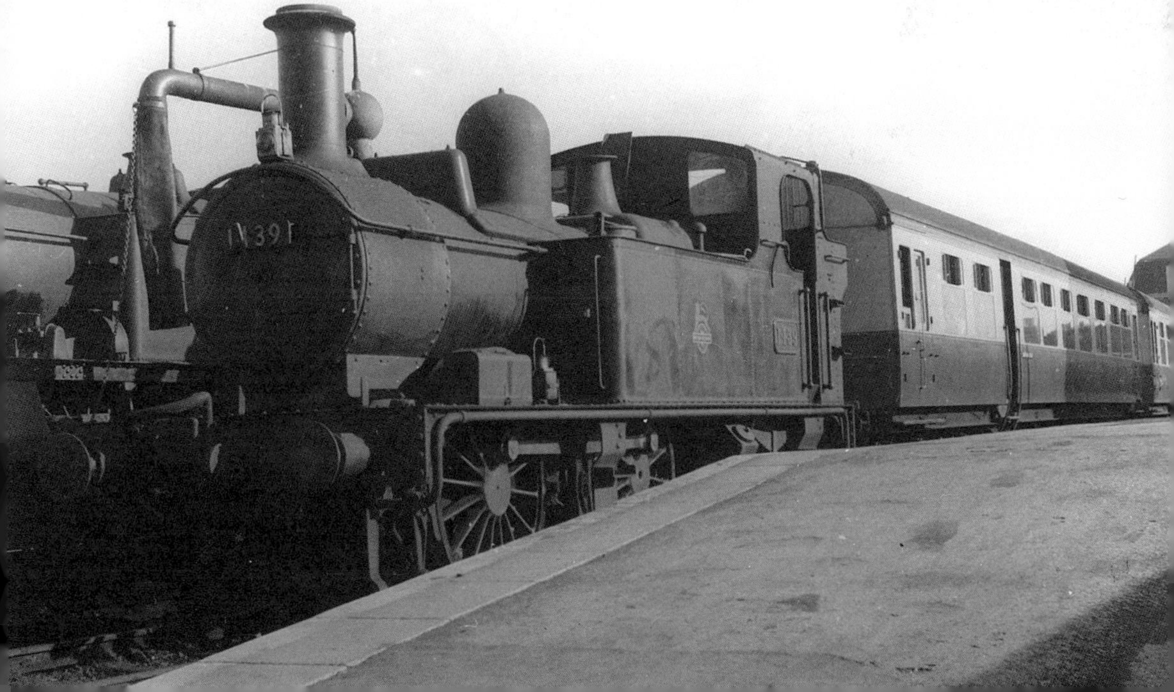

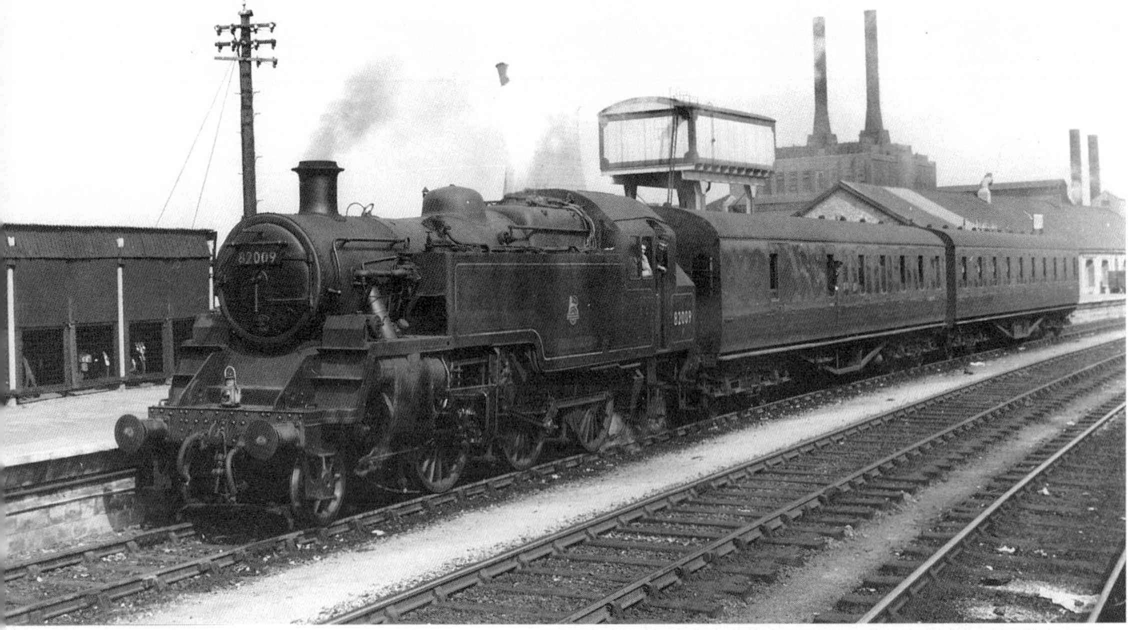
82009
82009

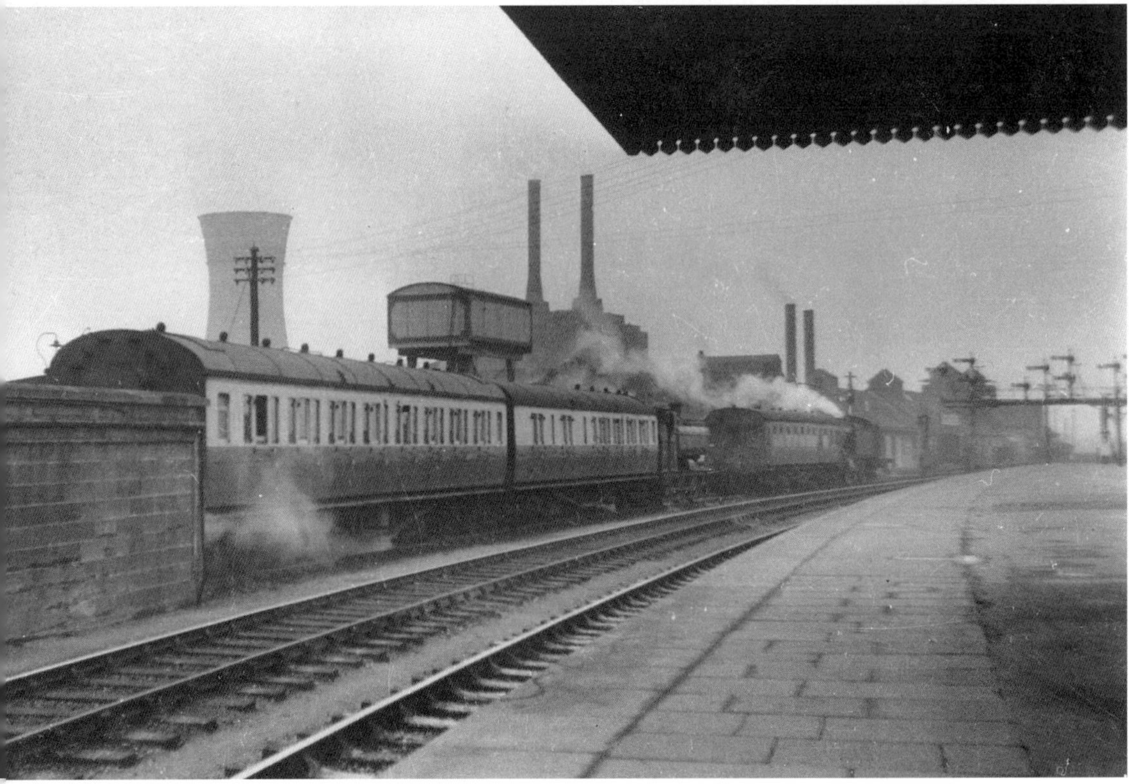

6. Less typical of branch line motive power is BR class 3 2-6-2T no. 82009, a type that was introduced in 1952. It is seen from the up main platform, soon after arrival on 1st September 1955. The power station is in the background; it had six sidings between 1928 and 1968. (N.L.Browne)

7. About to depart on 15th March 1958, a cold and gloomy day, is the 4.25pm to Moretonhampstead, formed of no. 4145 and an autocoach. Behind is the 4.35 to Exeter via Heathfield, which was headed by 0-6-0PT no. 7716. (M.Dart)

8. No. 5533 is being prepared to haul the final Teign Valley up train, the 8.0pm on 7th June 1958. The sidings on the left were taken out of use in August 1962 and Motorail trains began using the bay in 1967. (M.Dart)

9. A few minutes later, the locomotive was coupled to the specially lengthened train of six coaches. Two had sufficed on earlier trips that day. Note that the locomotive is outside the starting signal, which is occupied by a photographer. (M.Dart)

10. The final scheduled train to leave the bay platform was the 8.15pm to Moretonhampstead on 28th February 1959. Unlike the locomotive in the previous picture, 2-6-2T no. 4117 was shining brightly. Its train of four coaches carried the usual group of mourners. (M.Dart)

11.   Before station redevelopment could start, the goods shed (on the fold of the map under pictures 1 and 2) had to be demolished. A new goods yard with 12 sidings was developed parallel to the branch. It opened on 12th June 1911 and is seen on 28th August 1980, as no. 08238 approaches the main line (visible in the background) with ball clay from Heathfield. Whitelake Bridge can be seen beyond the middle tank wagon. (D.Mitchell)

12.   The 12-lever Newton Abbot Goods signal box stood close to the river from 1911 until 1926. The box was replaced by a ground frame, which was in use until 1972, when the connection was removed. No. 31273 was recorded with a Heathfield clay train on 26th March 1982. (D.Mitchell)

13. The redundant goods yard was used to store obsolete "clay hoods" in December 1982. While this design of wagon had been an improvement on the type that needed manual sheeting, more modern vehicles were being introduced. Goods traffic had ceased in 1970. (D.Mitchell)

14. A few minutes after picture 12 was taken, the train passed under the main road to Exeter and stopped opposite Watts Blake Bearne siding. This had been provided for Newton Abbot Clays Ltd in 1937. (D.Mitchell)

15. One mile north of the goods yard were Teignbridge Sidings. This southward view in 1982 reveals that they comprised two loop lines. They were first used by W.H.W.Williamson on 14th June 1892, although they were laid in 1890. (D.Mitchell)

16.　　At the north end of the sidings was a crossing keepers cottage, which was condemned in 1947 and subsequently renovated. Seen in 1982, it had lost its ground frame in 1965. The platforms were used for loading ball clay. (D.Mitchell)

TEIGNGRACE

The tiny community did not warrant a station but one was provided at the insistence of the Lord of the Manor of Stover. The drive to Stover House begins opposite the station approach road. The Stover Canal was used in connection with the Haytor Tramway, which conveyed granite from quarries on Dartmoor.

S.B

Station

Locks

ttage

rders

ce

Tr.

L.B

St Mary's Church

(Rectory)

School

STOVER CANAL

207 1 519

Teigngrace	1903	1913	1923	1933
Passenger tickets issued	4808	3519	3125	1234
Season tickets issued	*	*	-	-
Parcels forwarded	1551	1009	387	691
General goods forwarded (tons)	1	4	19	1
Coal and coke received (tons)	187	133	-	-
Other minerals received (tons)	174	305	273	-
General goods received (tons)	91	83	30	9
Trucks of livestock handled	-	-	-	-

(* not available)

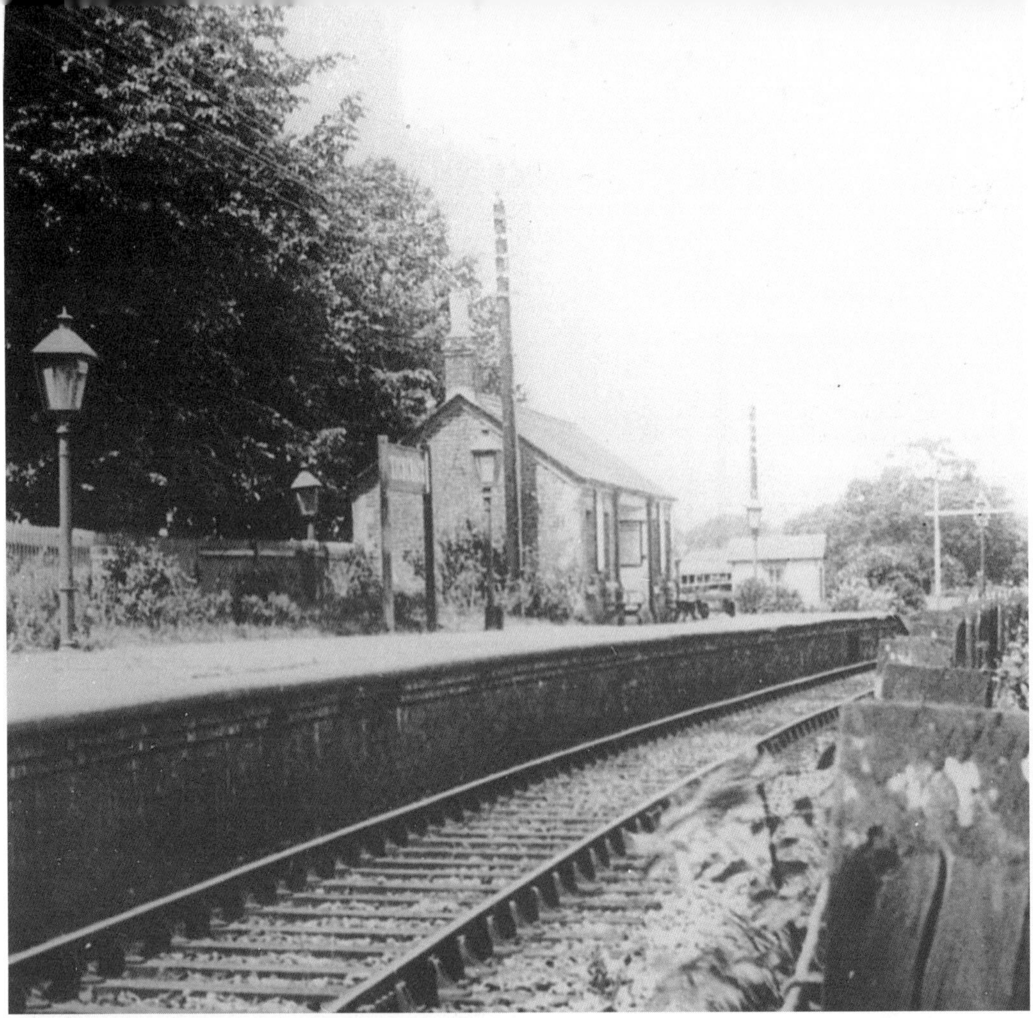

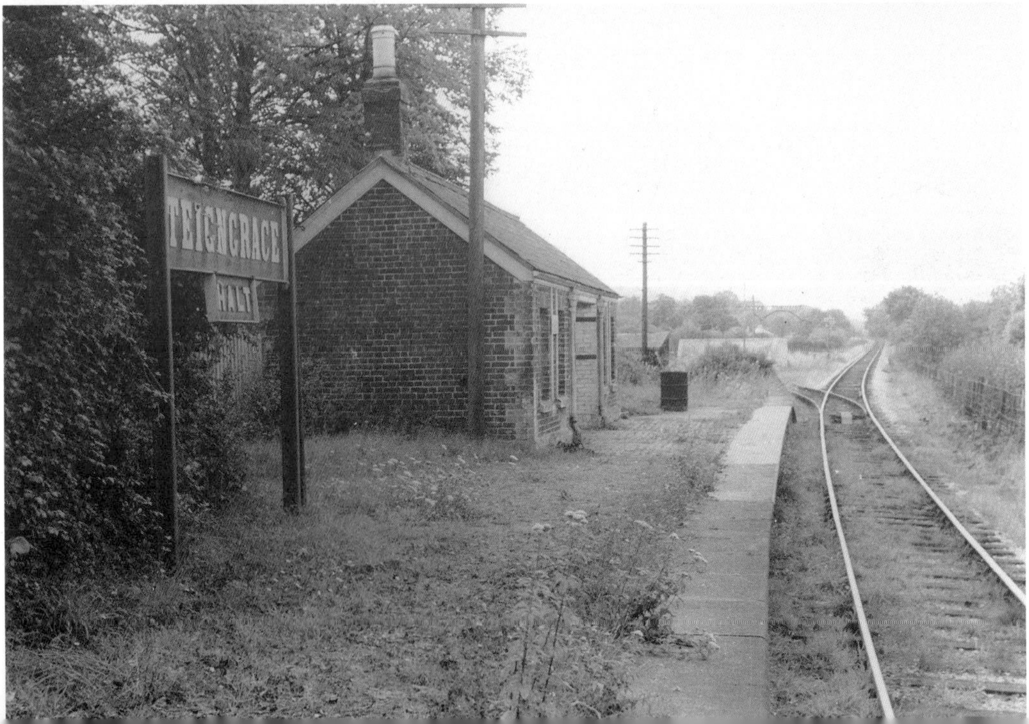
TEIGNGRACE
HALT

17.   The small oil-lit station saw few passengers and was closed as a wartime economy measure from 1st January 1917 to 1st May 1919. Seen in 1921, the building was boarded up following withdrawal of staff on 8th May 1939. (Lens of Sutton)

18.   The single siding was sometimes used for the loading of ball clay and was closed on 28th May 1962. There had once been an 11-lever signal box at the far end of the platform, which was photographed in about 1960.
(Lens of Sutton)

19. Evidence of the Haytor Tramway still survives on Dartmoor, although this photograph was taken in 1955. The granite was simply shaped to guide the wagon wheels, the grooves being of 3ft 6ins gauge. (D.Cullum)

SOUTH OF HEATHFIELD

20.   A loop siding had been provided in about 1913 for the loading of timber, but when photographed from the road bridge south of the station in 1957, it was used for loading ball clay. (D.Cullum)

21.   All regular traffic to Heathfield ceased in 1996 but the branch was reopened when bagged ball clay was loaded into two Cargowagons on 28th May 1998. No. 37674 is seen working a similar but longer train one month later. (D.Mitchell)

Heathfield
Station

Our route from Newton Abbot is on the right of this 1905 map, the line to Moretonhampstead is on the left and the Exeter track is at the top. The connection was for individual wagons only until 1907. The lack of a direct connection was rectified on 2nd October 1916. On the left is the Great Western Potteries & Brick Works, formerly Candy's. Its siding was in use from 1887 to 1966.

22. This northward view shows the pre-1916 layout and signal box. The map confirms the position of the 25-lever 1882 box. The station was named "Chudleigh Road" until 1st October 1882, just prior to it becoming a junction. (Lens of Sutton)

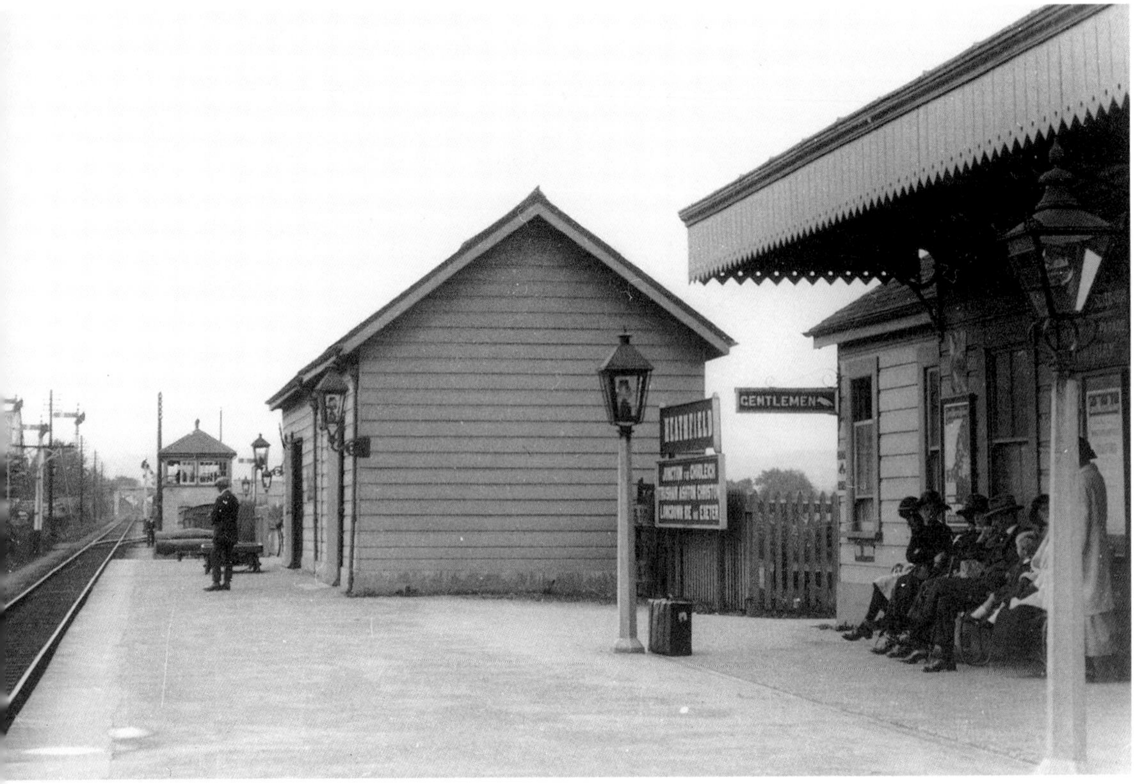
GENTLEMEN

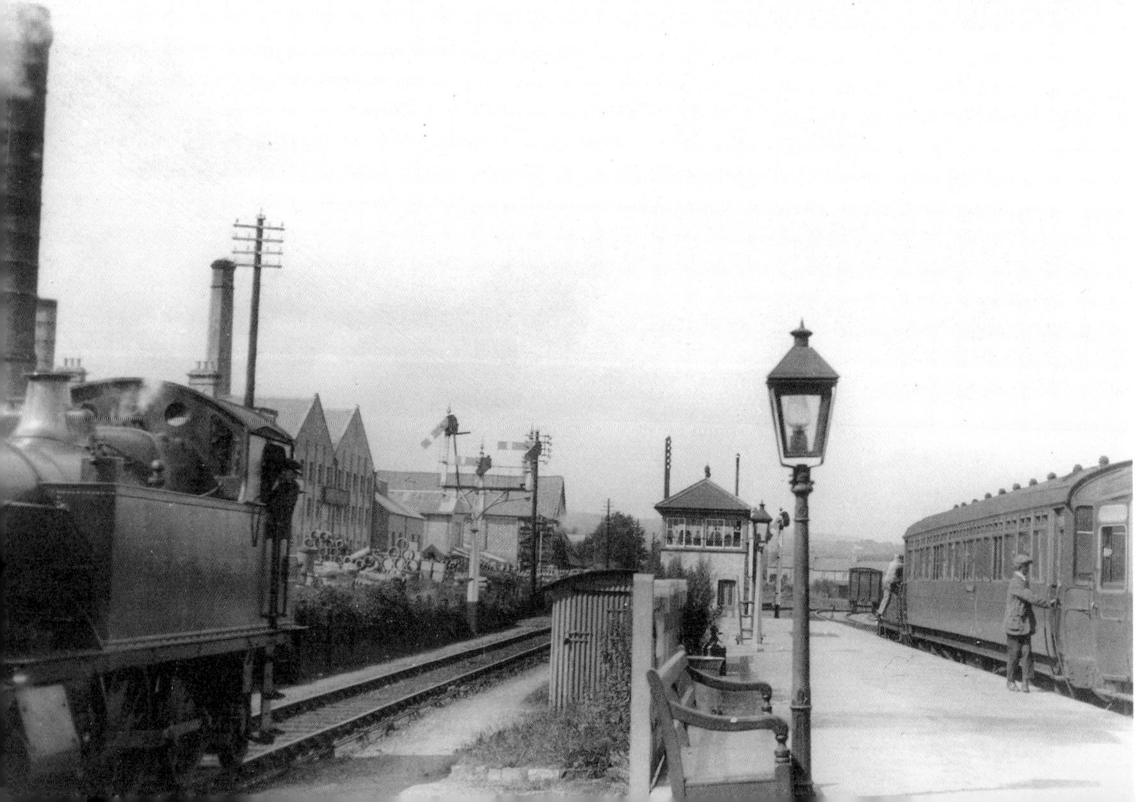

23.   A small crowd waits for an up train, which has been signalled from the 1916 box. The oil lamps gave a meagre light, hence their close proximity to one another. (Lens of Sutton)

Heathfield	1903	1913	1923	1933
Passenger tickets issued	12344	11575	13346	20719
Season tickets issued	*	*	61	84
Parcels forwarded	1699	2042	2992	2059
General goods forwarded (tons)	3582	4573	5115	4931
Coal and coke received (tons)	261	1017	3644	2353
Other minerals received (tons)	13171	10687	3364	670
General goods received (tons)	482	688	1153	1250
Trucks of livestock handled	-	1	1	-

(* not available)

3rd-SINGLE   SINGLE-3rd

5615   CHUDLEIGH to   5615

Chudleigh   Chudleigh

Heathfield   Heathfield

HEATHFIELD

5615   (W)   6d. H   FARE   6d. H   (W)   5615

For conditions see over For conditions see over

24.   A photograph from the early 1920s shows that there was still only one line (left) for Moretonhampstead trains. Two autocoaches wait to leave for the Teign Valley Line. The platform on the left was extended to the signal box in 1927. (Lens of Sutton)

25. A new platform (right) and passing loop for down Moretonhampstead trains came into use on 24th May 1927, allowing branch trains to pass here. Both lines were signalled for reversible running until 1943. "Metro" class 2-4-0T no. 3590 is seen on 22nd July 1939. (G.N.Southerden)

26. Two coaches depart for Moretonhampstead as a few passengers proceed towards the single coach of the Exeter service in September 1955. They were permitted to cross the tracks on the level.

The bay siding crossover was moved further away from the buffers and the loop lengthened in 1927. The crossover was removed in 1943. (N.L.Browne)

GENTLEMEN

5164
HEATHFIELD
JUNCTION FOR CHUDLEIGH
TRUSHAM ASHTON CHRISTOW
LONGDOWN IDE AND EXETER

27.   From 1927 to 1943, there was only a single connection from Exeter. This was doubled in May 1943, as seen in this 1957 photograph. The loop had been extended in March 1943, as seen in picture 20, and a crossover was provided. This was removed in 1970. (D.Cullum)

| BRIT. RLYS. (W) Tour 2 For day of issue only TOTNES TO CHUDLEIGH By RAIL via Heathfield THIRD CLASS For Conditions See Back | Brit. Rlys. (W) Tour 2 For day of issue only Dartmouth TO TOTNES By River Dart SteamboatCos Steamer Chudleigh | BRIT. RLYS. (W) Tour 2 For day of issue only CHUDLEIGH J TO DARTMOUTH By RAIL via Heathfield THIRD CLASS For Conditions See Back |

28.   An informative signboard still greeted passengers from Moretonhampstead in February 1957. Built in 1930, 2-6-2T no. 5164 avoided the scrapmen and can be found on the Severn Valley Railway today. (J.W.T.House/C.L.Caddy)

29. A well laden lad leaves the Moretonhampstead train on the same wet day, as passengers join a Teign Valley service in its penultimate year. Minimal shelter made this an inhospitable location in Winter. (J.W.T.House/C.L.Caddy)

30.   We gain a good view of the 1927 down platform and its waiting shelter as 0-4-2T no. 1429 waits with an Exeter train on 13th August 1957. It is hauling a former main line corridor coach. (R.E.Toop)

———————▶

31.   Wagons and materials occupy the bay platform during the final nine months that the other two were still in use. The length of the loop is apparent; it had been extended as part of a wartime scheme to improve the line as a diversionary route in the event of blockage of the coastal route. (Lens of Sutton)

———————▶

32.   The signal box was photographed in 1965, by which time the boards of the passenger crossing had been removed. The 42-lever frame was increased to 58 in 1927 and ceased to be used after October 1965. The number of levers in use was reduced from 53 to 44 in 1943. (C.L.Caddy)

33.   General goods traffic ceased on 14th June 1965, but coal traffic continued until 4th December 1967. A picture from 28th August 1980 shows no. 08238 about to reverse empty wagons into the siding seen in picture no. 21 and no. 47079 returning from the oil depot described in caption 35. (D.Mitchell)

34.   The "Devonian Rail Tour" was a joint RCTS/SEG trip from Waterloo to Paignton on 30th April 1983; the DEMU from the London-Hastings line made an unusual sight on the branch. On the right is the banana store of Geest Industries, which was rail served from April 1963 until December 1975, although the siding was laid in 1961. (D.Mitchell)

35.   An oil distribution terminal was opened by Gulf Oil, west of the station, on 10th October 1966. No. 60081 arrives at the Heltor Terminal on 13th December 1995 and is about to make the penultimate trip before closure of the sidings. The last empties left on 17th January 1996. (D.Mitchell)

36.   Hertfordshire Railtours used a newly-painted HST on a trip from London to Buckfastleigh on 26th April 1997 and, during its layover there, it operated a local excursion to Heathfield. There was little to interest your author (V.M.) on the site, only a few sanitary fittings. (D.Kelland)

BRIMLEY HALT

37.   The halt opened on 21st May 1928, but was devoid of lighting when photographed on 1st March 1956. New houses nearby had brought additional passengers in the fnal years of the line. (R.M.Casserley)

38.   A down goods train headed by 0-6-0PT no. 9671, clatters past on 7th September 1960. Seats and sign remain in place, although the last passenger had left more than 18 months previously. (C.L.Caddy)

BOVEY

Bovey	1903	1913	1923	1933
Passenger tickets issued	38297	34646	28754	14546
Season tickets issued	*	*	113	180
Parcels forwarded	11947	14384	12347	15316
General goods forwarded (tons)	1636	2200	1563	968
Coal and coke received (tons)	6493	3435	1438	668
Other minerals received (tons)	3797	5213	1334	1315
General goods received (tons)	3339	4518	3938	2787
Trucks of livestock handled	3	5	4	6

(* not available)

S.P

S.B

Post

Goods
Shed

Station

Post

S.P

Post

M.P

S.P

Pludda

The station was built about half a mile west of the centre of Bovey Tracey, on a road that was to become the B3344. This 1905 map shows a trailing connection to the goods yard from the down line. South of the station there were sidings on the west side of the line for Bovey Pottery and Bovey Granite.

39.   An undated postcard features a typical saddle tank locomotive entering the down platform, which had been added in 1893. Note the lack of weather protection in this area of high rainfall. The station name was always simply "Bovey". (Lens of Sutton)

40.   The generous space between the tracks was a legacy from the broad gauge days before 1892. The rails had been laid on longitudinal timbers; the same design was retained during the narrowing and is illustrated here. (Lens of Sutton)

41.   A 1921 view includes bullhead rail in chairs, which had replaced the old bridge rail by that time. A neatly valanced canopy had brought some protection for waiting passengers. One or two trains terminated here each day, particularly between the wars. (Lens of Sutton)

42.   The GWR was quick to recognise that road transport of the motorised type could be used for tourism and to link small communities with their stations. The vehicle on the right is destined for Bovey, Becky Falls and Manaton. (Lens of Sutton)

43.   Haytor Rocks were (and are) a popular site and a spectacular sight on Dartmoor. The three AECs were built by the Associated Equipment Company, successful bus builders in Southall for many decades. However, the vehicles illustrated were termed "charabancs". (Lens of Sutton)

44.   The goods yard connection can be seen ahead of this capacious train and the two-ton goods shed crane can be spotted near the passenger's hat. Hanging flower baskets add to this interesting record. (Lens of Sutton)

45.   The building on the right was occupied by a firm of agricultural engineers and a four-ton capacity crane was provided nearby for loading wagons in the yard. (Lens of Sutton)

46.   A southward view in 1955 includes the foot crossing for passengers and the level crossing for the road to Manaton. The track rises at 1 in 66 beyond it. The down platform had been extended northwards and a new signal box built (as seen) in about 1894. (D.Cullum)

47.   As can be seen from the signals in the background of the previous picture, reversible working of the up platform was possible. No. 1466 is bound for Moretonhampstead in February 1959. (J.W.T.House/C.L.Caddy)

48.   Freight and coal traffic withdrawal dates are the same as those at Heathfield. However, no. D6310 was photographed on 1st April 1969. The line was used to Bovey until 1970 for traffic from United Molasses of Avonmouth. (J.M.Tolson/F.Hornby)

49.   The exterior was photographed on the same day, when the buildings were in commercial use. Official closure was on 6th July 1970; on the previous day the 3000 or so local residents had their last chance to travel when a 5-car DMU made four return trips from Newton Abbot. (J.M.Tolson/F.Hornby)

PULLABROOK HALT

50.   The halt opened on 1st June 1931 and was named Hawkmoor until 13th June 1955, although Hawkmoor Hospital was some distance away. The idyllic scene was recorded in August 1955. (D.Cullum)

51.   January 1965 and the sign collectors had still not visited this remote site. The last freight train had passed by nine months earlier. (C.L.Caddy)

LUSTLEIGH

The station never had more than the single siding shown on the 1905 map.

Lustleigh	1903	1913	1923	1933
Passenger tickets issued	16898	16986	19710	13458
Season tickets issued	*	*	64	126
Parcels forwarded	4376	5834	3492	2567
General goods forwarded (tons)	675	494	785	278
Coal and coke received (tons)	456	13	114	68
Other minerals received (tons)	799	592	209	277
General goods received (tons)	402	506	400	307
Trucks of livestock handled	-	-	-	-

(* not available)

52.   The small signalbox seems to have had a short and unrecorded life; the directors of new lines were often required to make excessive signalling provisions. Here is further evidence of the early "baulk road". (Lens of Sutton)

53.   An early but indifferent view includes a horse and carriage in the station drive. The village of about 600 souls was situated nearby in a spectacularly beautiful valley. (Lens of Sutton)

2nd · SINGLE   SINGLE · 2nd
BOVEY to
Bovey   Bovey
Lustleigh   Lustleigh
LUSTLEIGH
(W)   6d.   FARE 6d.   (W)
For conditions see over For conditions see over

54.   A fine view from the nearby road in 1955 includes a camping coach. The first to appear here was in 1934 but all were withdrawn for the duration of World War II. They provided a cheap holiday for a large family in fine rural surroundings. (I.D.Beale)

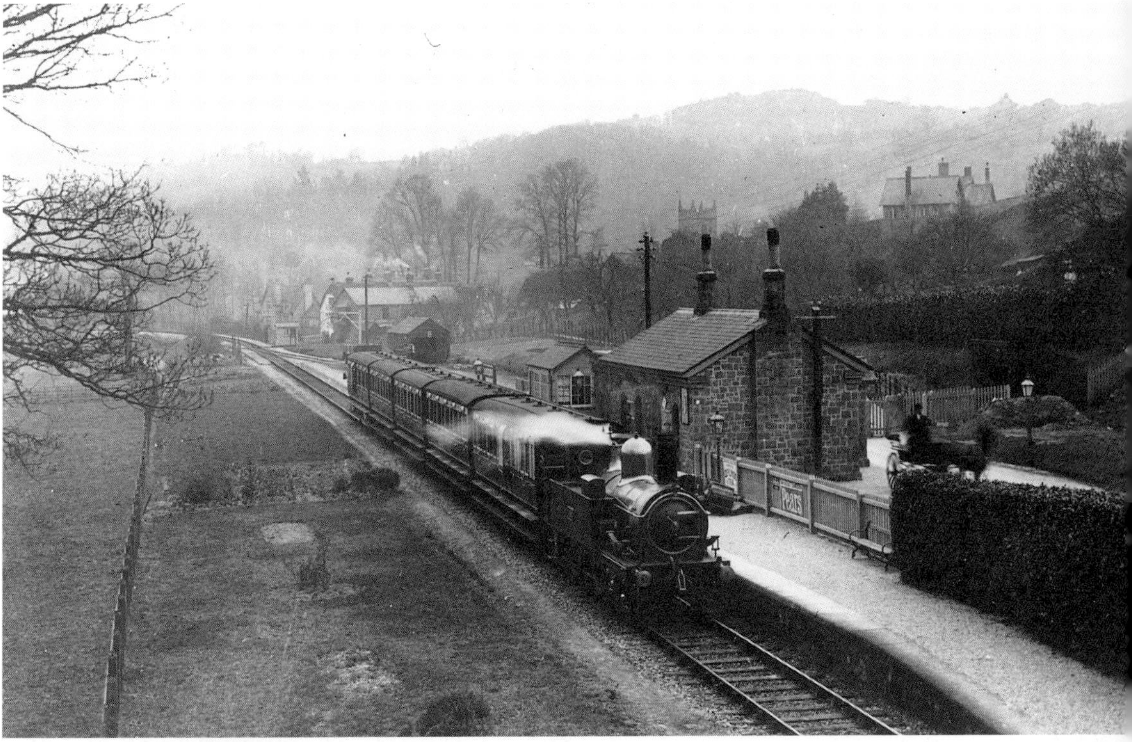
Pears

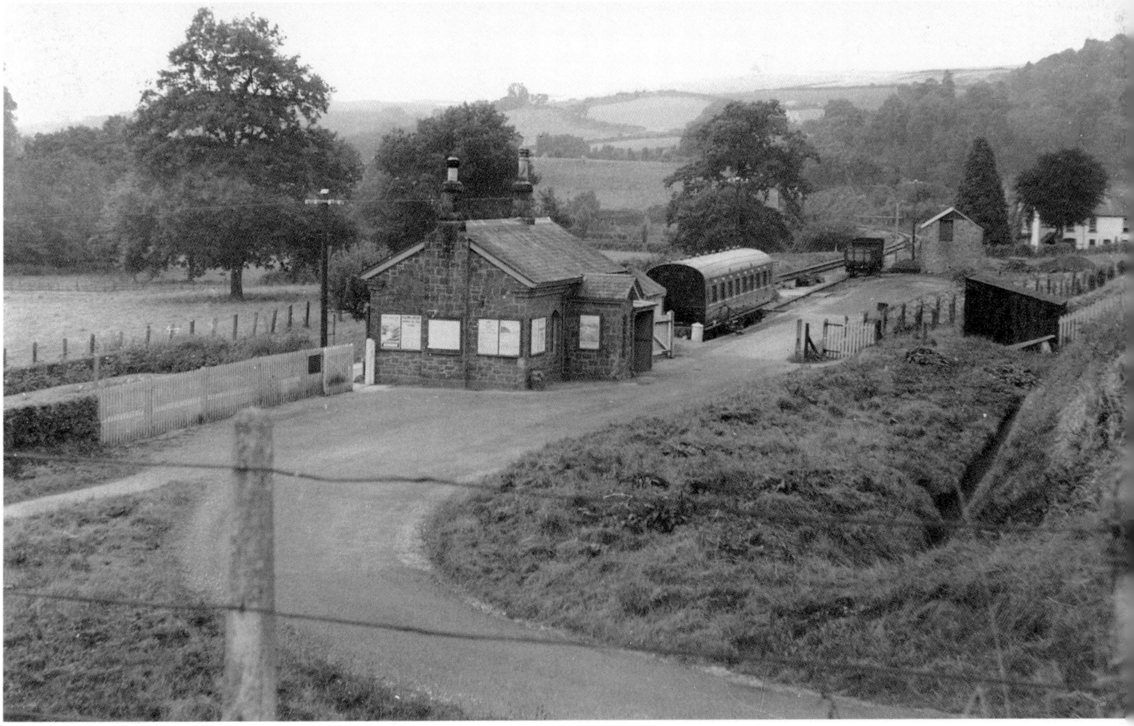

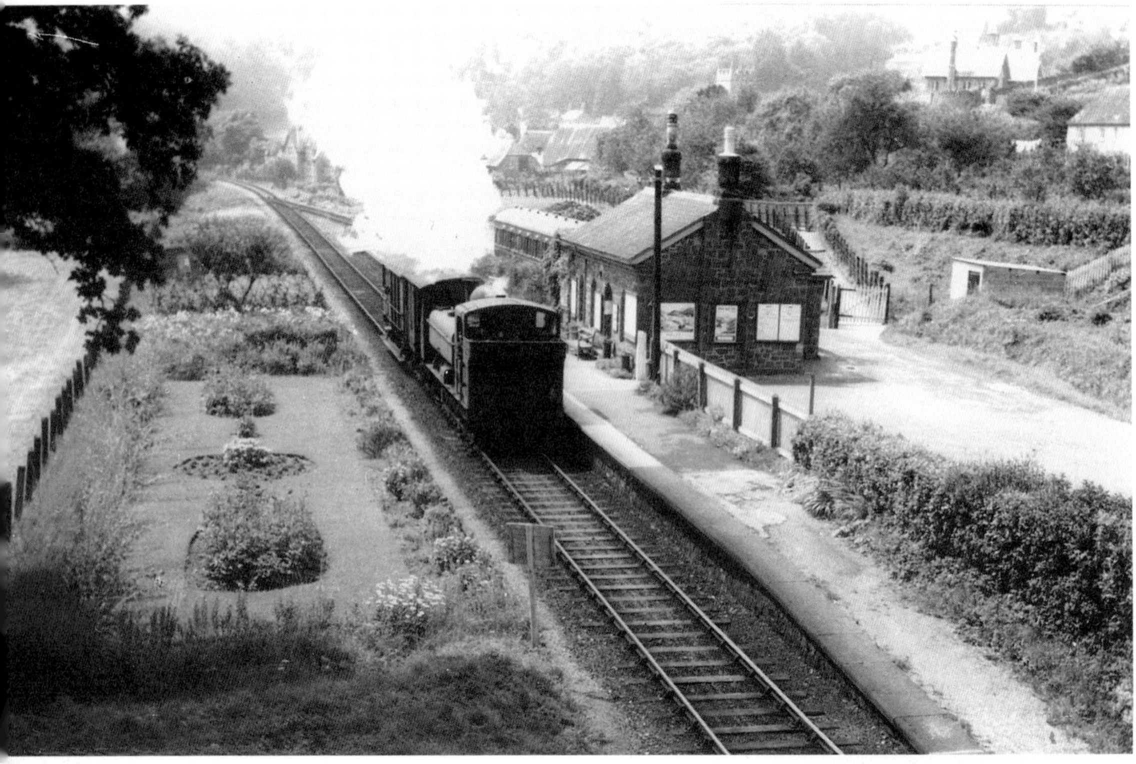

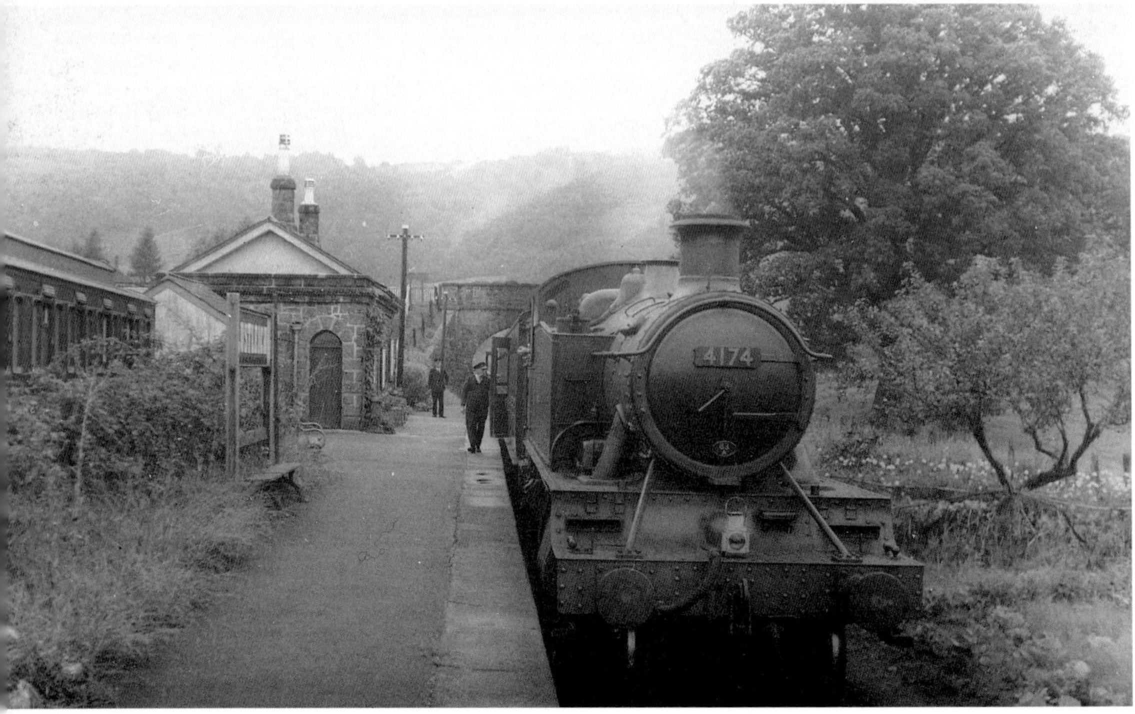
4174

55.   The land purchased for a possible loop was put to good use by green fingered railwaymen. No. 3600 is working freight from Newton Abbot on 19th July 1957. Goods traffic ceased on 6th April 1964, when the line closed completely. (D.Cullum)

3rd-SINGLE   SINGLE-3rd

996   CHILD

Moretonhampstead to
Moretonhampstead   Moretonhampstead
Lustleigh   Lustleigh
LUSTLEIGH

(W)   3½d H FARE 3½d H (W)
For conditions see over For conditions see over

996   CHILD

56.   There was an air of neglect when 2-6-2T no. 4174 was photographed on 21st August 1958, closure being anticipated by that time. Note that an elderly camping coach remained to the end. (A.E.Bennett)

57.   The steps in the background gave a short cut to the highway. After a long period of decay, the building was converted to a dwelling and it still serves that purpose today. (Lens of Sutton)

58. Approaching milepost 9 on 9th July 1957 is 0-6-0PT no. 3600 with the 7.0pm train from Moretonhampstead. The frequent change from cutting to embankment gave a rich variety of attractive vistas. (D.Cullum)

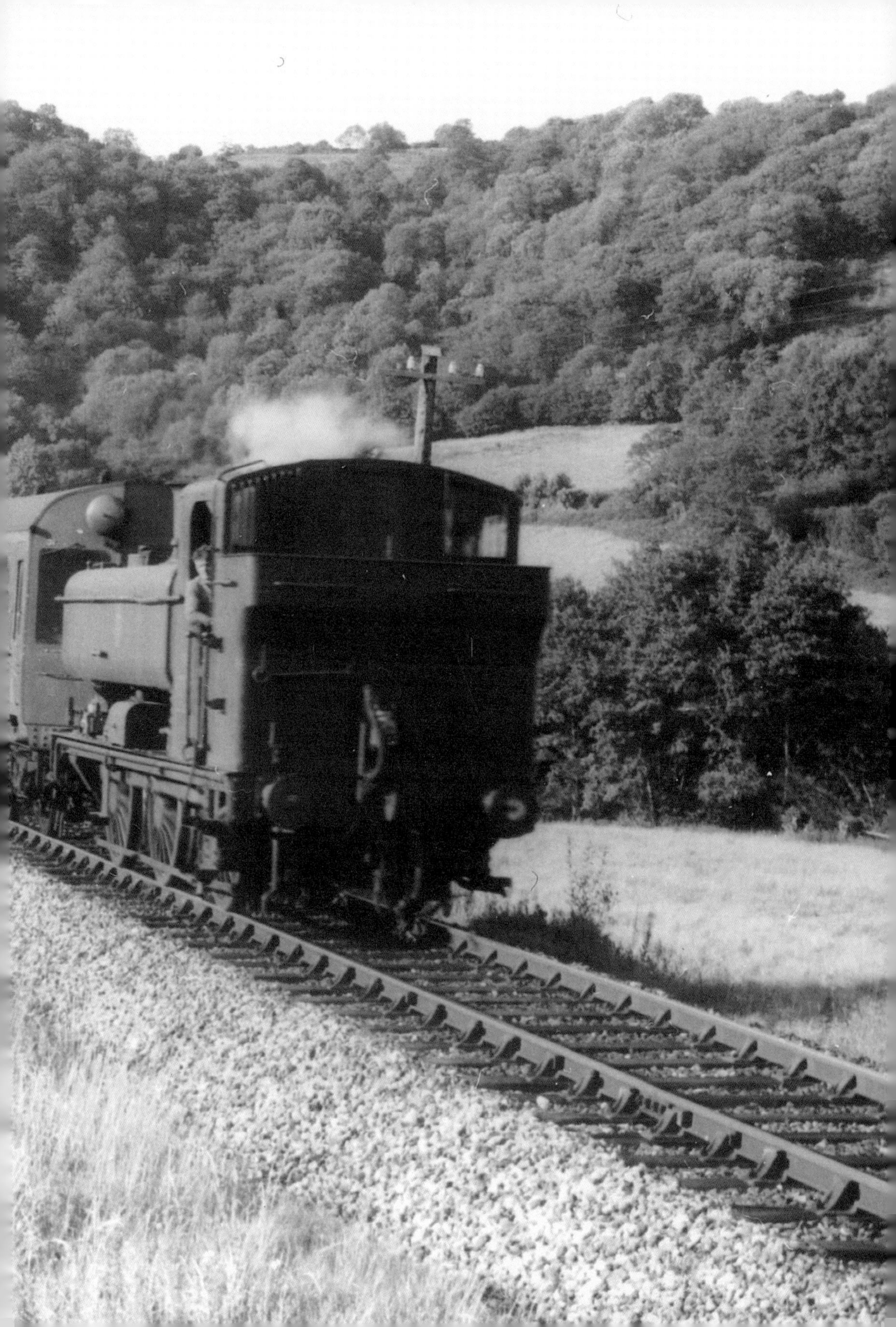

MORETONHAMPSTEAD

Courtenay Terrace

M.S { Moretonhampstead. ¼
Bovey Tracey 6¼

erminus

Goods Shed

S.P.

Engine House

Ga
Wo

S.

North of the station and parallel to the railway on this 1905 map is the main road between Bovey Tracey and Okehampton, now the A382. The gas works never had its own siding. Note that access to the goods yard was from the loop, thus avoiding another facing point on the passenger line.

59.   Four, six and eight wheeled coaches are evident in this postcard view, which probably dates from around 1910, as an early bus appears to be standing in the station yard. The "Prairie" 2-6-2Ts went into branch use soon after their introduction in 1906-07. (Lens of Sutton)

60.   Looking towards the end of the line, we can appreciate the rural setting of the station. Note the presence of the original type of track and the minimal platform lighting. (Lens of Sutton)

61.   The cattle dock was often found to contain Dartmoor ponies and was constructed from former broad gauge bridge rails. On the left of this 1921 photograph is a cattle wagon and the wooden shed that served as a garage for GWR's local fleet of buses. (Lens of Sutton)

2nd · SINGLE   SINGLE · 2nd

Moretonhampstead to
Moretonhampstead Moretonhampstead
Lustleigh   Lustleigh

LUSTLEIGH

(W)   8d.   FARE   8d.   (W)
ForConditions see overForConditions see over

62. This memorial stone was photographed in 1935 and stood near the pedestrian entrance until 1958. It was erected by the son of one of the directors in 1924. (M.Dart coll.)

63. The engine shed is seen in 1936 and was in use as such until 28th November 1947. Sliding doors were unusual on such a structure; maybe they were considered safer at this wind-prone upland location. (W.A.Camwell/M.Dart)

64.   This photograph, together with those numbered up to 73, were all taken in 1955, when branch line closures were becoming common, although in the pre-Beeching era. BR class 3 2-6-2T no. 82032 is about to depart at 3.15pm on 11th August. (D.Cullum)

65.   Ex-GWR types, such as no. 3659, were still active on the branch that year, although the control equipment on the autocoaches was not always in working order. Note their retractable steps, which, theoretically, could be used at remote locations.
(J.W.T.House/C.L.Caddy)

66.   On the right is the coal shed of Neck & Son and in front
of that is the weighing machine and its attendant hut.

Railwaymen's allotments feature on the left side; they are conveniently bisected by a stream. (I.D.Beale)

67.   The signal box was built onto the side of the engine shed in 1893, following the regauging. The box would have reduced ice formation on the cranks, in additon to facilitatng window cleaning. (I.D.Beale)

68.   The goods shed was of generous proportions, sufficient to house a road vehicle. It also contained a crane of 2-ton capacity. On the left is the goods office and the hut in the right foreground housed the gas meter. (I.D.Beale)

69.   The centre part of the roof had originally been glazed, but after World War II this area was largely covered over, leaving a small gap for smoke dispersal. Double doors to the right of the sheeted weighing machine led to the booking hall. Gentlemen had to pass through the arch on the right - their door was on the end of the building and is visible in picture 74. (I.D.Beale)

70.   The crane was of six-ton capacity and was often used for loading timber. The felted-over van body was a feed store until 1956, when it was broken up. (I.D.Beale)

71.   There had been a canopy over the entrance door (centre) until the early 1950s. The forecourt had been used by GWR buses until 1929, when Western National took over the two routes. Chagford was served from 1906 and Princetown from 1909, the latter usually only in the Summer. (D.Cullum)

Gt Western Ry   Gt Western Ry
Moretonh'pst'd   Moretonh'pst'd
TO
HAWKMOOR HALT
THIRD CLASS
1/0 Z   Fare   1/0 Z
Hawkmoor   Hawkmoor
FOR CONDITIONS SEE BACK (W.L

425   425

Moretonhampstead	1903	1913	1923	1933
Passenger tickets issued	30292	47666	28323	12099
Season tickets issued	*	*	163	212
Parcels forwarded	16553	20716	15550	19941
General goods forwarded (tons)	2185	2165	3709	1398
Coal and coke received (tons)	1399	557	626	595
Other minerals received (tons)	2158	1906	2026	982
General goods received (tons)	5109	5572	4328	2779
Trucks of livestock handled	202	324	307	114

(* not available)

72.   The wash-down apron for cattle trucks could be seen to the end; railwaymen were pleased to see this dirty traffic diminish. On the left is the lamp hut; oil was always kept remote from other buildings. (D.Cullum)

73.　The track was kept tidy to the end, in both senses of the word, although the well fertilised track on the left was prone to generate weeds very rapidly. (I.D.Beale)

74.　A driver has time to pose as he makes his way to the peace of the driving cab, where his coat hangs unattended. Autocoach working was steadily phased out during the mid-1950s, as more diesel units were planned. (Lens of Sutton)

The GWR adapted a nearby country house as a hotel in 1929; its 1934 advertisement is shown here. The building became a hospital during World War II.

75.   A gas light stands intact, while weeds take hold in every crevice. The structure had many features in common with the terminus at Ashburton, which is still standing. Easy comparison can be made by reference to our *Branch Line to Ashburton*. (Lens of Sutton)

76.   The smoke staining of the gable end reveals that some repair work had taken place. Passengers were usually left to alight in the open if the locomotive had to run round. No. 5154 is doing so on 29th September 1956. (H.C.Casserley)

77.   Seen a few minutes later, the locomotive is close to the water column. Water was often taken here but coal was obtained at Newton Abbot after 1947. A turntable had been situated just beyond the white-painted permanent way hut until about 1913. (H.C.Casserley)

78.   A solitary soul approaches the train, which is well down the platform on 21st August 1958. The coaches were kept on the loop road in the train shed at night, while the locomotive ran light to and from Newton Abbot. The town of about 1500 inhabitants made little use of its railway in its final years. (A.E.Bennett)

79.   The melancholy scene in 1965 includes the later feedstuffs store (on stilts), the enginemens lobby and the east doorway of the shed, which had been boarded up for about 20 years. Both goods and engine sheds were retained by a road transport firm, the latter eventually achieving a listed building status. Freight by rail ceased on 6th April 1964, but parcel traffic continued by road until 1st January 1965. Part of the yard, together with the engine shed, was used by then as a coal store by the Co-op. (C.L.Caddy)

2. Teign Valley Line

CHUDLEIGH KNIGHTON HALT

80.   The halt was opened on 9th June 1924 and was a little over one mile from Heathfield, on the north side of the line. Beyond the A38 road bridge in the background, three sidings were laid on Knighton Heath for the Ministry of Works in 1943. They were closed in 1949 and lifted about three years later, having only been used for a few months in 1944 for canned petrol for the US Army involved with the Normandy landings. The original timber platform was replaced after the war, as seen. (Lens of Sutton)

CHUDLEIGH

Chudleigh Bridge

Ashburton..8½ M.S

Chudleigh
Station

L.B+

Heightley Cotta

Heightley Bridge

Corn Mills
(Disused)

S.B.

Cr.

Chudleigh	1903	1913	1923	1933
Passenger tickets issued	15496	19895	7100	2695
Season tickets issued	*	*	27	20
Parcels forwarded	5645	10034	7975	4767
General goods forwarded (tons)	133	667	175	129
Coal and coke received (tons)	1997	602	538	320
Other minerals received (tons)	1236	4102	1573	171
General goods received (tons)	1360	2212	1844	1326
Trucks of livestock handled	-	4	-	1
(* not available)				

The dots represent the centre of the River Teign on this 1905 edition. The road crossing the map became the A38, but its recent widening has almost obliterated the site. The station was prone to flooding and so a supplementary platform ws built near the top border of the map in the mid-1920s, so that railmotors could terminate there.

81.   Details include three and a half passengers awaiting the Exeter train, cases outside the goods shed, two staff members in attendance, part of the 13-lever signal box, the wooden crane and five four-wheeled coaches hauled by a class 517 0-4-2T. The box functioned as a ground frame from 1893 until 1910 and was dismantled in about 1930. (Lens of Sutton)

82. Most passengers defected to the buses after they commenced on the main road in 1919. The occupants of the camping coach in this 1956 picture would have had a tranquil location for their holiday. (R.M.Casserley)

83. After passenger services ceased in 1958, one man was retained to supervise freight and parcel traffic, the latter being conveyed by road. The platform canopy had long gone by the time that this photograph was taken in 1963. (C.L.Caddy)

84. The man in charge used the office on the right of this 1965 picture. Although general freight ceased that year, oil and coal were unloaded here until 4th December 1967. Coal was subsequently concentrated at Exmouth Junction. (J.P.Alsop)

The 1905 edition shows the original short loop.

85.   A goods loop was added in the foreground of this picture in 1911 and it was greatly extended southwards in 1943. The narrow valley was particularly beautiful in this area. (Lens of Sutton)

86. The economy of construction of the buildings is evident in this view from the bridge seen in the previous picture. Four four-wheelers appear with a class 517 0-4-2T. The 13-lever signal box was built in 1882. (Lens of Sutton)

87.   Three post-World War II views include the long loop opened on 8th July 1943, together with the associated platform. The signal box was erected in 1911 and had 25 levers. Crockham Quarry is in the background. (Lens of Sutton)

Trusham Station

G.P.

Trusham Quarry
(Disused)

Trusham	1903	1913	1923	1933
Passenger tickets issued	5111	9377	9833	8269
Season tickets issued	*	*	40	27
Parcels forwarded	865	1760	1796	1191
General goods forwarded (tons)	291	730	955	648
Coal and coke received (tons)	259	271	254	489
Other minerals received (tons)	16	338	862	474
General goods received (tons)	175	724	821	353
Trucks of livestock handled	-	1	-	-
(* not available)				

S.Ps

ocombe Bridge

L.B

S.P

S.B.

S.P

W.M.

S.Ps

B3193

S.P

M.P

Cro B

Conv

W.M

arries

Teign Valley Concrete Works

The 1936-39 survey features the long loop of 1911 and, to the east of it, the loop siding for Trusham Quarry, in use between 1912 and 1931. It remained in place until 1943. It is interesting to note that the B3193 crosses the Crockham Quarry sidings between the concrete works and the quarry. These lines were usable from 1904 to 1968. The 1912 station masters house is top left.

88.	Milk was loaded at most Devon stations but seldom in this unauthorised manner. The yellow brick building survives as a dwelling. The 1946 platform shelter is obscured by the milk churns. (Lens of Sutton)

89.	The loop became a siding in June 1958, when the signal box was downgraded to a ground frame. The loop was reinstated in 1960, albeit shorter at its north end. The box closed completely in 1961 and the goods yard followed on 5th April 1965, the line towards Exeter having been lifted in February 1962. (Lens of Sutton)

About 600yds north of the station was Whetcombe Quarry siding, which was open from 1910 to 1931 but remained in situ until 1952. It is seen on the 1939 edition.

Spara Bridge

Cottages

ASHTON

Stone

Crane

S.B.

Well

Engine Shed

B r a m

Ashton	1903	1913	1923	1933
Passenger tickets issued	6192	6872	7261	5695
Season tickets issued	*	*	24	30
Parcels forwarded	2671	2414	1487	1123
General goods forwarded (tons)	593	404	353	71
Coal and coke received (tons)	258	57	118	15
Other minerals received (tons)	1505	355	477	254
General goods received (tons)	1298	636	247	120
Trucks of livestock handled	29	-	1	-
(* not available)				

The 1905 map shows the engine shed, although it closed in 1903. The signal box (S.B.) was in use until May 1920; it had 17 levers and was not a block post after 1893. A carriage shed had once stood at the southern end of the shed road.

90. The staff comprised a station master and a porter until 1929; thereafter there were just two porters, on shifts. The oil lamps were eventually replaced by the brighter pressurised Tilley type. The shed contained a porters room, coal store and lamp room. (Lens of Sutton)

91. The scenic delights are evident as a train arrives from Exeter. A camping coach was situated here from 1934 to 1939. Note the lack of cab backplate on the class 517 tank engine.
(Lens of Sutton)

92.   The water tank in the background of this 1921 photograph was removed in 1928, when supplies were provided at the adjacent stations. Two of the levers (left) worked distant signals and the other was for the gate bolt. (Lens of Sutton)

93.   Two locomotives were allocated to this shed during the period of the line's isolation; there was only one from 1892 until 1st July 1903. The two-ton crane is on the left of this 1949 photograph. The shed stood for a further ten years. (A.J.Pike/F.Hornby)

94.   Beyond the crossing was a siding on the east side of the line to Ryecroft Quarry, but it was only in use from 1930 to 1939. Seen in September 1960, the line closed at the end of that month, following flooding, although official closure was not until 1st May 1961. (C.L.Caddy)

CHRISTOW

Christow	1903	1913	1923	1933
Passenger tickets issued	5417	14480	16115	11592
Season tickets issued	*	*	24	94
Parcels forwarded	815	3277	3691	2845
General goods forwarded (tons)	508	1508	1310	306
Coal and coke received (tons)	109	215	275	122
Other minerals received (tons)	282	424	225	451
General goods received (tons)	396	2383	2055	650
Trucks of livestock handled	18	76	67	33

(* not available)

During the years that Ashton was the northern terminus (1882-1903), there was an extension, known as Teignhouse Siding, which ended at the boundary fence marked at the bottom of this 1905 map. Subsequently, stone was loaded at the sidings shown here.

95.   This was the most important station on the route and was the only one at which passenger trains could pass one another until 1943. Here we see a locomotive running round a one-coach terminating train and also the five-ton crane in the goods yard. (Lens of Sutton)

96.   An inter-war picture helps to show that little changed in this vicinity. The oil lamps were eventually replaced by Tilley lamps on hoists. The down loop was extended northwards 370yds in 1943, as part of the upgrading of the route for diverted trains. (Lens of Sutton)

97.   Five photographs from August 1949 reveal further details. The 1928 water tank is evident above the goods shed roof as 4300 class no. 5321 waits with a down freight on the up line. This probably was to allow a down passenger train to overtake it. (A.J.Pike/F.Hornby)

98.   The waiting shelter appears to date from 1903, but the water column was not added until 1928, when stone shunting activity had increased considerably. Two sidings had been laid behind the platform in 1914 for the Scatter Rock Quarry traffic. (A.J.Pike/F.Hornby)

99.   The prospective passenger's perspective was not impressive but then stone was the most important source of revenue here. There is evidence of an extension northwards since picture 95 was taken. (A.J.Pike/F.Hornby)

100.   The goods shed window was partially occluded by the extension and subsequently by a poster board. The up side water column is also visible. All freight traffic ceased on 30th September 1960, following flood damage to the track. (A.J.Pike/F.Hornby)

101.   Looking north from the station we see the 1925 loading plant of Scatter Rock Macadams Ltd (centre), one of two sidings that passed behind the signal box, and the goods yard (left). From this, a three quarter mile line curved away sharply to the Bridford Quarry of the Devon Basalt & Granite Company from 1910 to 1931. It passed over a level crossing and was worked by two different 0-4-0STs. The one mile long aerial ropeway of 1914 passes over the tracks. It conveyed crushed material from Scatter Rock Quarry for loading or coating as tarmac. The old established Bridford Barytes Mine once produced lead ores but with the advent of the railway, its barium sulphate output was conveyed (initially via Newton Abbot) to Exeter for milling. It increased greatly in the 1930s, offsetting a reduction in stone traffic, but ceased in July 1958. It was usually loaded at one of the up sidings and was used mainly in white paint. (A.J.Pike/F.Hornby)

102.   Trailing from the down loop is one of the two lines to the goods yard. The 1903 signal box remained in use unaltered until passenger trains were withdrawn in 1958, when it was downgraded to a ground frame. It had a 30-lever frame. The steps from the down platform were a late addition and can be seen in the background. (Lens of Sutton)

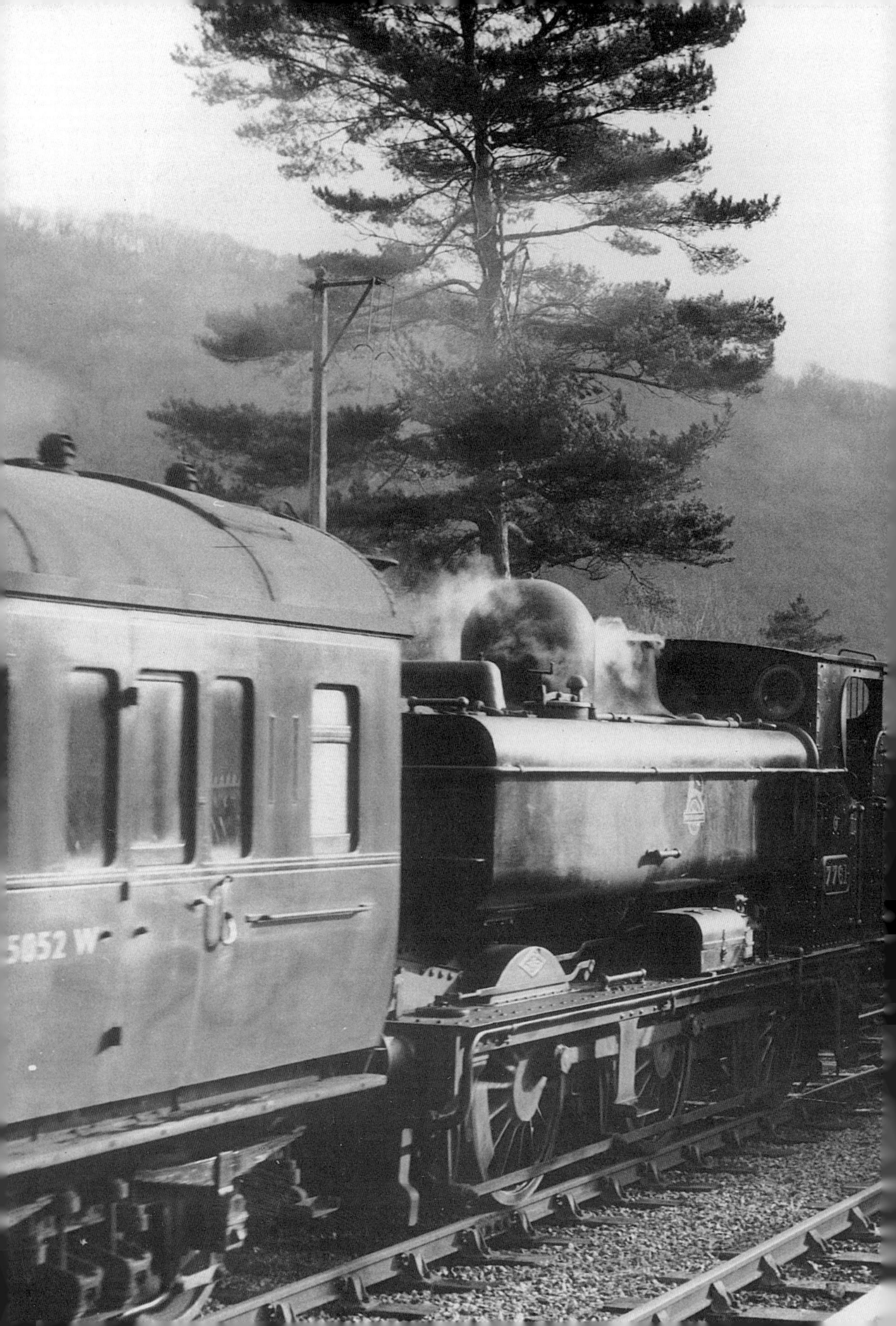
5052 W

103.　　The time is 1.20pm on 18th January 1958 and the railwaymen may be contemplating their future. No. 7761 is running in with the 12.45 Exeter to Newton Abbot as no. 1469 waits with the 12.40 from Newton Abbot. The red-brick building became a dwelling. (P.W.Gray)

DUNSFORD HALT

104.   The timber edged platform came into use on 16th January 1928 and was on the south side of the line. Replaced by concrete after World War II, the halt was almost two miles from the village it was purported to serve. (Lens of Sutton)

LONGDOWN

105.   The signal was added in 1906, along with an extra lever in the ground frame, left. It was extremely unusual in being in mid-section; station staff had to telephone Christow to ensure that the line was clear before clearing it. A five-lever signal box was added in 1916, this facilitating the return of banking engines. (Lens of Sutton)

Longdown	1903	1913	1923	1933
Passenger tickets issued	2789	5359	5058	1826
Season tickets issued	*	*	22	56
Parcels forwarded	110	565	413	245
General goods forwarded (tons)	42	97	12	13
Coal and coke received (tons)	16	-	50	18
Other minerals received (tons)	160	127	249	80
General goods received (tons)	16	89	149	25
Trucks of livestock handled	-	-	-	-

(* not available)

The single loop siding was used for little else than coal for, and timber from, the Culver Estate. It ceased to be used after 18th November 1956 and all the land eventually reverted to the estate after line closure.

Longdown Station

F.P.

Aqueduct

106.   The station was located one mile from the village in extensive woodland, with the 248yd long Culver Tunnel to the west and Perridge Tunnel, 836yds in length, on the Exeter side. A new 9-lever frame was installed in the signal box (left) in 1943 in connection with a down loop, which was in use between 19th September 1943 and 20th July 1954. There were also three ground frames and the single line instruments were in the booking office. The up line had been signalled for reversible running. (Lens of Sutton)

IDE

Vicarage

St. Ida's Church
(Vicarage)

THE GREEN

Bearsdene

Grave Yard

Canns House

F.P.

Station

M.P.

F.P.

B

Pyr

The 1905 edition reveals the simple arrangement that was never altered. After the heavily forested areas near the summit of the line, we enter more open agricultural land on the descent into the Exe Valley.

107.   The building was similar to others on the route but there was never a signal box here. However, a camping coach graced the siding for the Summers of 1935 to 1939. (Lens of Sutton)

108. The suffix *HALT* was added on 1st October 1923, when manning was reduced to mornings only. No.1451 approaches the lampless platform, whose former passengers found buses much more convenient, particularly at the Exeter end of the journey. (A.Luxton/M.Dart coll.)

109. Staffing ceased on 7th March 1955 and freight facilities were withdrawn on the same day. The remains of the dock are seen not long before total closure. The site was subsequently developed for bungalows. (Lens of Sutton)

Ide	1903	1913	1923	1933
Passenger tickets issued	5276	7782	7819	7149
Season tickets issued	*	*	6	26
Parcels forwarded	190	1797	557	806
General goods forwarded (tons)	62	441	227	59
Coal and coke received (tons)	5	52	10	45
Other minerals received (tons)	26	1208	633	59
General goods received (tons)	23	190	136	77
Trucks of livestock handled	-	-	-	1
(* not available)				

ALPHINGTON HALT

110. Opened on 2nd April 1928, the original timber structure remained in use until line closure. Steam railmotors of this type were introduced to the route in 1923 and were displaced by the locomotive hauled/propelled autocoach in about 1935. On some Summer Saturdays in the 1950s, one train from Newton Abbot terminated here and passengers continued to Exeter by bus, as St. Davids was so busy with holiday trains in the middle of the day. (G.N.Southernden)

June - September 1955 timetable

EXETER, CHRISTOW and HEATHFIELD
(Third class only)

Week Days only

Miles		am	am	am	am		am	am		pm	pm	pm	pm	pm	pm	pm	pm	
				Saturdays only	Saturdays only		Except Saturdays	Saturdays only		Saturdays only	Saturdays only	Except Saturdays	Saturdays only	Except Saturdays	Saturdays only		Saturdays only	
	Exeter (St. David's).. dep	6 30	7 0	9Z34	..	..	9 44	11Z50	..	..	12Z41	1245	..	4 25	4 53	6 5	9 30	..
1	„ (St. Thomas)	6 34	7 4	9Z41	..	..	9 49	11Z56	..	..	12Z48	1250	..	4 29	5 3	6 10	9 33	..
2	Alphington Halt	6 38	7 9	9Z46	9 54	..	9 54	12Z 1	..	12 5	12Z53	1255	1258	4 34	5 10	6 14	9 38	..
3¼	Ide Halt	6 42	7 14		9 58	..	9 58		..	1210		1 1	1 3	4 39	5 15	6 19	9 43	..
6	Longdown	6 49	7 22		10 6	..	10 6		..	1218		1 10	1 12	4 47	5 23	6 27	9 51	..
7¼	Dunsford Halt	6 53	7 26		10 9	..	10 9		..	1222		1 14	1 16	4 52	5 27	6 31	9 55	..
9¼	Christow	6 58	7 33		1015	..	1015		..	1228		1 28	1 28	4 58	5 35	6 43	10 0	..
10¾	Ashton	7 4	7 38		1019	..	1019		..	1233		1 32	1 32	5 4	5 39	6 48	10 5	..
12¾	Trusham	7 10	7 44		1025	..	1025		..	1239		1 40	1 40	5 10	5 45	6 53	1012	..
14¾	Chudleigh	..	7 49		1029	..	1029		..	1244		1 45	1 45	5 15	5 50	6 58	1017	..
16	Chudleigh Knighton Halt	..	7 53		1033	..	1033		..	1248		1 48	1 48	5 19	5 54	7 2	1021	..
17½	**Heathfield** arr	..	**7 57**		**1038**	..	**1038**		..	**1253**		**1 55**	**1 55**	**5 24**	**6 0**	**7 8**	**1026**	..
21¼	90 Newton Abbot .. arr	..	8 25		1050	..	1050		..	..		2 7	2 7	5 46	..	7 34	1036	..

Week Days only

Miles		am	am	am	am		am	am	am		pm	pm	pm	pm	pm	pm			
			Except Saturdays	Saturdays only	Saturdays only		Except Saturdays	Saturdays only	Saturdays only		Saturdays only	Saturdays only	Except Saturdays	Saturdays only					
	90 Newton Abbot .. dep	..	7 50	7 50		..	1032	1032		..	1244		3 0	3 15	6 5	8 15	..	..	..
—	**Heathfield** dep	..	8 5	8 5		..	1045	1050		..	1 3		3 15	3 25	6 20	8 30	..	..	..
1½	Chudleigh Knighton Halt	..	8 10	8 10		..	1050	1055		..	1 9		3 20	3 29	6 24	8 34	..	..	..
2¾	Chudleigh	..	8 14	8 14		..	1053	11 0		..	1 13		3 24	3 34	6 28	8 38	..	..	..
4¾	Trusham	7 45	8 19	8 19		..	1058	11 4		..	1 20		3 29	3 40	6 33	8 43	..	..	..
6¾	Ashton	7 50	8 24	8 24		..	11 3	11 9		..	1 24		3 34	3 45	6 38	8 48	..	..	..
8¼	Christow	8 0	8 30	8 30		..	11 8	1115		..	1 30		3 39	3 52	6B55	8 53	..	..	..
10¼	Dunsford Halt	8 6	8 35	8 35		..	1114	1121		..	1 38		3 45	3 58	7 0	9 0	..	..	..
11½	Longdown	8 11	8 40	8 40		..	1118	1126		..	1 43		3 50	4 3	7 5	9 5	..	..	..
14¼	Ide Halt	8 17	8 46	8 46		..	1125	1132		..	1 50		3 56	4 10	7 12	9 10	..	..	..
15½	Alphington Halt	8 21	8 50	8 50	8Z55	..	1129	1136	11Z41	..	1 54	1Z59	4 0	4 14	7 16	9 15	..	..	..
16½	**Exeter** (St. Thomas)	8 27	8 55	..	9Z 0	..	1135	..	11Z46	..	..	2Z 4	4 6	4 21	7 24	9 22	..	..	..
17½	„ (St. David's).. arr	8 34	9 3	..	9Z 8	..	1140	..	11Z50	..	..	2Z 9	4 10	4 27	7 30	9 27	..	..	..

B Arr. 6 44 pm. Z By Exeter Corporation Omnibus (heavy luggage not conveyed)

EXETER CITY BASIN

The Basin (top right) opened in 1830 and was used by ships from London and Bristol for example. The South Devon Railway (diagonally across this 1905 map) opened a trailing siding from its down line to the Basin in 1867. Of dual gauge, trains composed of both types of stock could be seen working up the down line to and from St. Davids, as only this section had a third rail at that time. The completion of the line from Heathfield on 1st July 1903 resulted in the opening of the three lines radiating from the lower border of the map - left to Alphington Road Goods Depot, centre to St. Davids and right to the Basin. The latter was little used, as operationally it was more convenient to work wagons via the Riverside Yard, beyond St. Davids. On the left is the 33-lever City Basin Junction Signal Box (S.B.). It was replaced on 9th December 1962 by Exeter City Basin, which was a few yards nearer St. Davids. This in turn closed on 17th November 1986.

Works
(Exeter Corporation)

Saw Mills

HAVEN BAN

Engineering Works

G.W.R. BASIN BRANCH

Meter Factory

Devon Art Pottery

C. Railway

S.B.

Basin Junction

Filter Bed

218
1·402

A   Exeter Railway Junction
B   Alphington Road Goods Junction
C   Exeter Basin Loop Junction
D   Low Level Loop Junction
E   Exeter Basin Junction

	Sidings	Open	Closed
1.	Canal Basin	17-06-1867	06-09-1965
2.	Gas Works	05-11-1883	23-11-1973
3.	Electricity Works	02-03-1904	01-01-1963
4.	Oil Depot	07-11-1966	21-07-1983
5.	Kings Asphalt	24-06-1929	Before 1981
6.	Alphington Rd. Goods	01-07-1903	04-12-1967
7.	Cattle Market	26-07-1939	Before 1966
8.	Scrap metal, Marsh Barton	08-08-1958	In use 1998
9.	Cadbury Fry, Marsh Barton	31-12-1959	06-1970 (last used)

111.   Exeter Railway Junction is seen from the signal box on 26th June 1970, as no. D1012 passes with the 18.27 Paddington to Plymouth (Fridays only) train. The down branch line was removed on 21st January 1979. (D.Mitchell)

112.   Low Level Loop Junction is in the foreground as "Peak" diesel heads west on 30th April 1973. Behind the camera is Water Lane level crossing, seen in the next picture and in the centre of the 1905 map. The unusual square-ended distant signal served as a repeater for the junction signal, to aid drivers propelling empty oil trains onto the main line. (D.Mitchell)

113.   Turning round on the same day, we see the southern end of the loop and one of the points to the gas works sidings, which were removed in the late 1970s. The loading gauge has lost its hoop. There were two other level crossings - Haven Road and Tan Lane. (D.Mitchell)

114.   No. 08839 descends from the main line towards Low Level Loop Junction on 19th December 1989. It is hauling bitumen tankers for the Colas Roads Depot; the siding in the foreground was used for this traffic between about 1985 and 1990. (D.Mitchell)

115.   Scrap metal from the Marsh Barton yard of Pearse & Co. is behind no. 37717 on 7th July 1970, as it waits to join the main line and leave the last surviving part of the former Exeter Railway from Christow. In the foreground is part of the defunct Alphington Road Goods Dept. (D.Mitchell)

The right side of this map continues from the left of the previous one and shows most of the goods yard, together with the position of its 6-ton crane. The passenger station is at the top; this had housed the head office of the SDR.

116.   Being much closer to the city centre than St. Davids, this station was popular with passengers from the local villages that we have visited on our journey from Heathfield. This is a 1930s northward view of the structure which was opened on 30th May 1846. It lost the remains of its overall roof in 1971. (Stations UK)

St. Andrew's
Church

EXETER ST. DAVIDS

School
~wick Playground

St. Clement's Church
(Site of)   S.P

Cattle Pens

Goods Shed

S.P

Cr.

39

P.H.

Smy.

S.P

Engine Shed

St. David's Station

F.P.

W

S.P

S.P

S.P

S.P

S.P

M.P

S.P

M.P

We finish our journey by crossing the River
Exe (bottom), as the lines from London Waterloo
curve in on the right. The street tramway featured
on this 1905 survey is illustrated in *Exeter and
Taunton Tramways* (Middleton Press).

117. A southward view against the light in 1958 has our route from St. Thomas on the right and the steep curving incline to Exeter Central on the left. Opened in 1862 by the London & South Western Railway, it was standard gauge from the outset, hence the need for a third rail to the Basin. (D.Cullum)

EXETER, ASHTON, and HEATHFIELD (1st and 3rd class).—Great Western.

Miles	Down.	Week Days. mrn	mrn	mrn	mrn	aft	aft	aft	aft
	Exeter. St. David's......dep.	6 35	7 40	9 45	11 5	1 12	3 12	6 12	7 20
1	Exeter. St. Thomas..........	6 38	7 43	9 48	1110	1 15	3 15	6 18	7 23
3¼	Ide..........................	6 48	7 53	9 58	1120	1 25	3 25	6 28	7 33
6	Longdown.....................	6 57	8 2	10 7	1129	1 34	3 34	6 37	7 42
9¼	Christow.....................	7 7	8 11	1034	1138	1 44	3 46	6 48	7 51
10¾	Ashton.......................	7 12	....	1039	....	1 49	3 51	6 53	....
12¾	Trusham......................	7 21	....	1048	....	1 58	4 0	7 2	....
14½	Chudleigh....................	7 27	....	1054	....	2 4	4 6	7 8	....
17	Heathfield (below)........arr.	7 33	....	11 0	....	2 10	4 12	7 14	....

Miles	Up.	Week Days. mrn	mrn	mrn	aft	aft	aft	aft	aft
	Heathfield...............dep.	....	8 32	....	1222	3 18	6 15	....	9 20
2¼	Chudleigh....................	....	8 39	....	1229	3 25	6 22	....	9 27
4½	Trusham......................	....	8 45	....	1235	3 31	6 28	....	9 33
6½	Ashton.......................	....	8 51	....	1241	3 37	6 34	....	9 39
7¾	Christow.....................	8 22	8 57	1150	1247	3 45	6 47	8 5	9 45
11	Longdown.....................	8 32	9 7	12 0	1257	3 55	6 57	8 15	9 55
13¾	Ide..........................	8 40	9 15	12 7	1 5	4 3	7 5	8 23	10 3
16	Exeter. St. Thomas 22, 27 arr.	8 47	9 22	1215	1 12	4 10	7 12	8 30	1010
17	Exeter. St. David's 22, 27 "	8 52	9 27	1218	1 17	4 15	7 17	8 35	1015

April 1910

NEWTON ABBOT and MORETONHAMPSTEAD (1st and 3rd class).—Great Western.

Miles	Down.	Week Days. mrn	b	aft	aft	aft	aft	Sundays. mrn	aft
	Newton Abbot......dep.	8 13	9 50	12 5	3 0	5 50	9 0	8 45	7 55
2¼	Teigngrace.............	8 21	9 57	1212	3 7	5 58	9 8	....	....
3¾	Heathfield (above).....	8 27	10 3	1218	3 13	6 4	9 14	8 55	8 5
6	Bovey, for Ilsington...	8 34	1011	1225	3 20	6 11	9 21	9 1	8 11
8¾	Lustleigh..............	8 44	1021	1235	3 30	6 21	9 31	9 11	8 21
12¼	Moretonhampstead * arr	8 57	1034	1248	3 43	6 35	9 45	9 25	8 35

Miles	Up.	Week Days. mrn	b	mrn	aft	aft	aft	Sundays. mrn	aft
	Moretonhampstead.dep.	7 10	9 50	1045	1 50	3 55	7 0	7 45	6 55
3¾	Lustleigh.............	7 19	10 1	1054	1 59	4 5	7 9	7 54	7 4
6½	Bovey, for Ilsington..	7 27	1010	11 2	2 7	4 12	7 18	8 1	7 11
8¾	Heathfield (above)....	7 36	1017	11 9	2 14	4 20	7 24	8 7	7 17
10¼	Teigngrace.........[48	7 41	1022	1114	2 19	4 25	7 29	....	....
12¼	Newton Abbot 22, 27, a	7 47	1028	1120	2 25	4 31	7 35	8 17	7 27

b Wednesdays and Saturdays; also on the 4th Tuesday in the month. * Station for Chagford (4 miles).

Chagford.—Road Motors leave Moretonhampstead Station at 9 10 (Wednesdays only) and 10 40 mrn., 12 55, 3 50, and 6 40 aft. for Chagford.
Cars also leave Chagford for Moretonhampstead Station at 8 30 (Wednesdays only) and 9 50 mrn., 12 10, 3, and 6 aft.

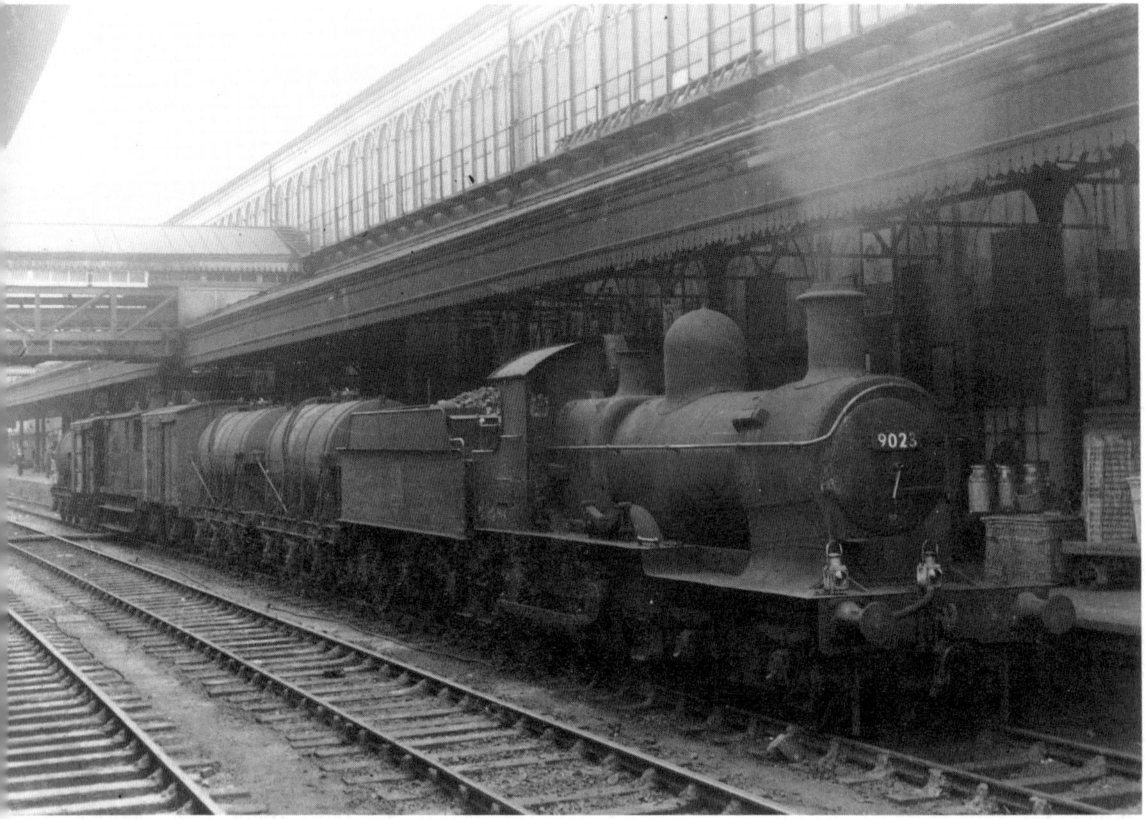
9023

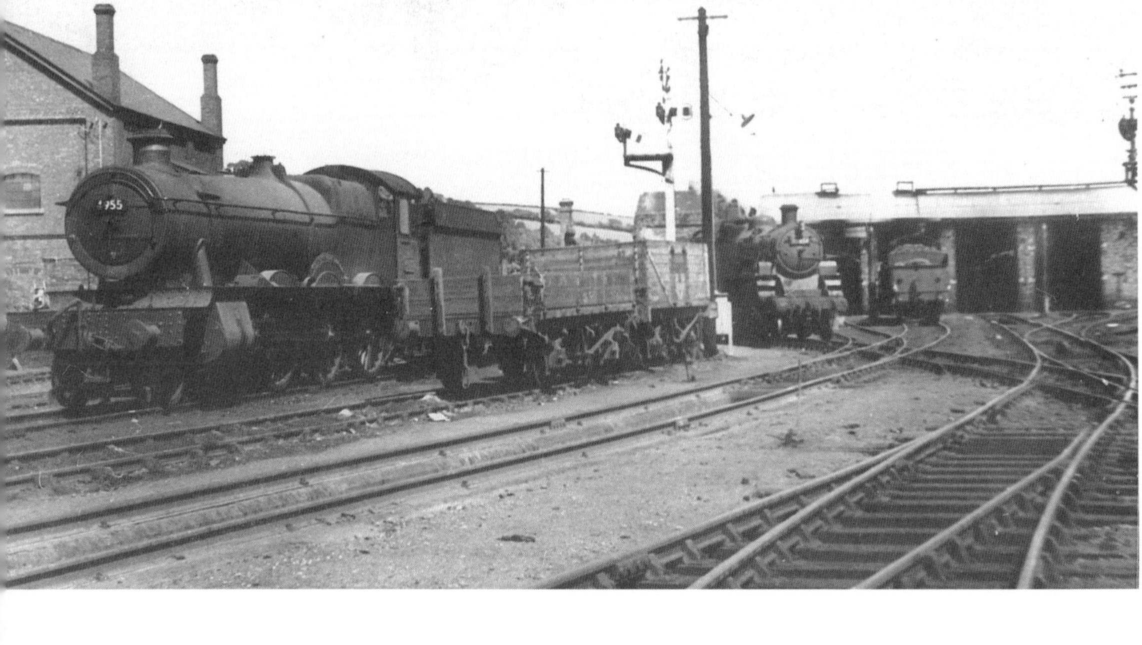

118.   Milk churns on the platform and milk tankers in the train serve to emphasise the importance of this perishable traffic in Devon. No. 9023 was one of the 9000 class of 4-4-0s introduced in 1936. (Lens of Sutton)

119.   A glimpse into the motive power depot in about 1956 includes no. 4955 *Plaspower Hall*. When trains were diverted via the Teign Valley, they were normally double headed to Newton Abbot by tender locomotives. (A.J.Pike/F.Hornby)

120.   We say farewell to the much loved route in the company of many mourners on platform 4 on 7th June 1958. Class 4500 2-6-2T no. 5533 was due to leave at 9.30pm with the last train, but it was delayed until 10.10 by the crowds involved in "funeral rites". The saddened passengers reached Newton Abbot one hour late. (M.Dart)

Other views of this station can be found in our
Exeter to Barnstaple **and** ***Exeter to Tavistock*** **albums.**

MP Middleton Press

Easebourne Lane, Midhurst, West Sussex.
GU29 9AZ   Tel:01730 813169

EVOLVING THE ULTIMATE RAIL ENCYCLOPEDIA

www.middletonpress.co.uk   email:info@middletonpress.co.uk
A-0 906520 B-1 873793 C-1 901706 D-1 904474

OOP Out of Print at time of printing - Please check current availability   **BROCHURE AVAILABLE SHOWING NEW TITLES**